# Tenko-Gami

Learn how to Create your very own

# Paper Flowers

Using Never Revealed Secrets.

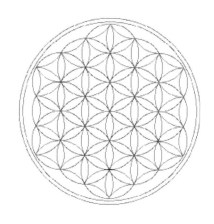

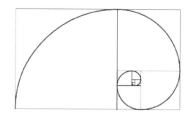

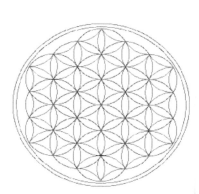

# Table Of Contents

# How It All Started

People always ask how I got started with flower making. It started as a hobby when I was selling cars a few years ago. There were times when my days seemed slow, but one day while waiting for some customers, I asked the Lord to help me support myself in a better way. The answer came soon after, in the form of a gift: a paper flower made from a napkin.

I started getting interested in paper flowers, and searched the internet to see what resources there were, but discovered there was nothing that gave clear directions on how to make them. I didn't realize this was my answer, not right away anyhow. I began experimenting on how to create flowers with paper, and over time, became better at this art form. I finally had a gift and a goal, which is to transform plain pieces of napkins and tissues into a replicated flower. My friends say I followed my calling. You could say I found a way to help others. Now I'm on a mission to make a difference one flower at a time.

I had help building my talent by researching how the classic artists, such as Michelangelo, Leonardo Da Vinci, and Fibonacci created their masterpieces. I then applied their principles and formulas to flower making. If you've ever seen my step by step guide, you'll notice that I start out with one petal, and leaf, and build from there, just like a painter will start with one layer, then add another, and another before the painting is complete. In the same way, I can show others how to make the flowers in an easy format.

The way I make my flowers is a simple process of tear, roll and wrap using your fingers and a little water for your fingertips. It takes some practice, but I believe anyone can learn this art.

I was hesitant at first to make a living creating flowers from paper, but after some thinking, realized it's okay to do something I love and earn money for it too.

I became curious when I started wondering what other people would create if they knew how to make paper flowers. What could result from the public knowing how to make something beautiful from simple tissues and napkins? The answers are limitless, like the imagination. I hope my Book Tenko-Gami will help you to create something uniquely your own.

Arnold World

# Many Uses:

There are numerous uses for World Paper Flowers. The Best Thing Is Soft paper towels are readily available in most rest rooms. Kitchens and fast food restaurants. However, sharing the miracle and giving a person a medium to express their creativity is why this publication was originally created.

# Start a New Hobby:

Create paper flowers in thirty minutes or less using paper napkins from restaurants, bars, coffee shops or you can just buy some at one of your local dollar store.

Hobbies consist of dedicating some time and in most situations money to pursue a relaxing diversion. As far as cost Tenko-Gami is a very inexpensive hobby. The cost is minimal because all you need is to gain the knowledge for creating beautiful inexpensive flowers is contained in this writing. Along with some basic materials to create and store your project and some paper napkins which can be found almost anywhere at no cost other than the drink or meal you purchase.

# Great for arts & Craft Projects:

With a group of children that sometime find themselves rained in or just needing an indoor project that teaches creativity with out breaking the bank, Tenko-Gami is the perfect solution. Depending on the complexity of the tenko-Gami flower can easily keep a group of children busy for hours.

A simple bouquet can be assigned as an art and craft's school project. Creating World Paper Flowers Instill imagination, inspiration and ingenuity because like real flowers no two Tenko-Gami flower will ever be exactly the same.

# Fund Raisers:

With the cost of material at the time of this writing being about two dollars for twenty county two ply colors or white paper tissue napkins, even with the nominal cost of ten cents per flower, Tenko-Gami makes for a cost-effective fund raiser using the systems like auditions and bidding as well as raffles.

# First year Wedding Anniversaries:

Paper is the gift for year one for a wedding anniversary. Turn your wedding napkin into something memorable and unique. Knowing you made it with love in you heart will make the gift personal and special. Follow the instructions and present your love ones with a one of a kind gift.

# Here is a quick check off list:

_____List flowers to create
_____Design an event sign-up sheet
_____List event volunteers
_____Track event budget
_____Design a fund-raised flier
_____Design a pledge form for each flower
_____Track pledge made
_____Make a donation receipt
_____Track donation received
_____Share event photo's online

# Identify your group with matching flowers:

Flowers with multiple petals and leafs will enhance any ceremonial assembly. Your beautiful paper flowers will quickly identify the group.

# Perfect traveling gifts:

You only need a paper napkin and fifteen minutes to create the perfect traveling gift. Buying a gift can be a challenge under any circumstance but with Tenko-Gami you do not have to worry about cost of materials because tissue is easy to find. Due to the unlimited combination of flower and petal sizes and shapes along with a rainbow of color selections Tenko-Gami helps creates originality, imagination and developing a child's dexterity, nimbleness, agility and hand eye coordination.

# Inspirational & Educational:

A simple bouquet can be assigned as an arts and craft's school projects. Creating Tenko-Gami Flowers instill imagination, inspiration and ingenuity because like real flowers Tenko-Gami will never have two flowers that are exactly alike. With a group of children that sometime find themselves rained in or just needing an indoor project that teaches creativity with out breaking the bank, Tenko-Gami is a perfect solution.

Among the many findings of the recent study, the academic Value of Hands-On Craft Projects in elementary schools, the following stand out:

.Student learning improves when classroom lessons incorporate hands-on craft activities.
.Student behavior and socialization skills improve when crafts are undertaken.
.learning through craft projects accommodates students with different learning styles.
.In classes where teachers devoted a moderately large proportion of instructional time to craft projects, students achieved significantly higher scores on a test that required them to apply what they learned in a new context. Tenko-Gami Wants to help teachers integrate crafting in the curriculum, we can present your staff with ground-breaking education research, discuss teachers needs and introduce Tenko-Gami. Special resources for educators. We want to ensure that Tenko-Gami can provide all of the creative materials and ideals to assist teachers in researching students through creative and fulfilling projects.

# Parts Of A Flower

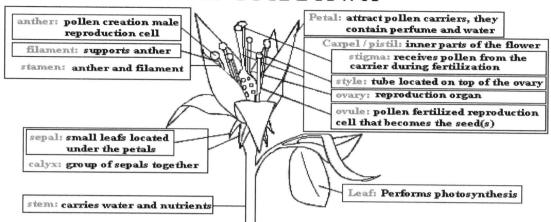

**anther:** pollen creation male reproduction cell

**filament:** supports anther

**stamen:** anther and filament

**Petal:** attract pollen carriers, they contain perfume and water

**Carpel / pistil:** inner parts of the flower

**stigma:** receives pollen from the carrier during fertilization

**style:** tube located on top of the ovary

**ovary:** reproduction organ

**ovule:** pollen fertilized reproduction cell that becomes the seed(s)

**sepal:** small leafs located under the petals

**calyx:** group of sepals together

**stem:** carries water and nutrients

**Leaf:** Performs photosynthesis

Difficulty Level: Beginners
Name: Mother's Choice
Description : 1 Petal, 1 Leaf, with stem
Time Challenge ( 10 Minutes)

Tenko-Gami.com

**Fun for all ages !**   No extra tools or material needed.

There are four additional words

## Find The Red Words

| w | a | f | i | l | o | m | e | n | t | b | d | r | e | d | e | c |
|---|---|---|---|---|---|---|---|---|---|---|---|---|---|---|---|---|
| f | o | v | a | r | y | f | g | s | t | i | g | m | o | q | b | l |
| l | u | r | v | z | w | a | P | i | n | k | e | f | v | h | l | n |
| o | o | z | l | r | s | t | y | l | u | c | x | g | a | i | u | w |
| w | a | h | l | d | t | y | e | l | l | o | w | j | r | o | e | o |
| e | n | s | f | x | P | e | t | a | l | h | l | o | i | r | a | r |
| r | s | t | i | g | m | a | i | s | e | P | a | l | e | a | s | h |
| a | t | e | l | u | y | n | P | j | a | g | r | e | e | n | t | x |
| n | y | m | a | k | z | t | e | e | f | y | i | e | P | g | a | w |
| a | l | z | m | l | y | h | d | w | r | s | o | l | u | e | m | h |
| t | e | s | e | e | d | e | u | k | x | f | n | u | r | P | e | i |
| o | q | t | n | u | r | r | n | j | d | m | l | v | P | t | n | t |
| m | a | n | t | h | u | v | c | a | l | y | x | o | l | i | q | e |
| y | b | l | a | c | k | c | l | f | a | c | g | e | w | b | u | l |
| i | z | d | c | a | r | P | e | l | m | n | v | o | n | e | P | u |
| f | l | o | w | e | r | a | n | a | t | o | m | l | x | y | r | z |
| v | e | s | P | i | s | t | i | l | P | u | r | P | l | e | r | s |

## Find The Different Colors

**Black**   Red   Yellow

White   Red   Green   Pink

Orange   Purple   Blue

**log into Tenko-Gami.com**

# Five Supplies that come in handy:

1. First of all you will need some paper tissue to create your flowers. As stated earlier paper tissue, the medium from which all of my flowers were created can be found almost anywhere.
2. Second, you are going to need a small box to keep the current project you are working on.
3. Third, you will need a wet paper napkin, wet towel or sponge to keep your fingers moist while you work on your project.
4. Fourth, A ball point pen or soft lead pencil will prove very useful when punching holes in your cup or writings the bottom of your napkin to create a time capsule moment captured.
5. Fifth, You will need a paper or foam cup to display your new creation and be used for a holding station while working on big projects.

# Paper tissue or napkin #1

The best thing is soft paper towels are readily available in most rest rooms, Kitchens and fast food restaurants. At the time of this writing the costs of materials are about two dollars for twenty count two ply colors or white paper tissue napkins. The minimal cost will be ten cents per flower, that's a small price to pay for hours of family fun.

## Paper tissue or Napkin

# Small Box #2

This is one of the important tools you can have as some crafts people who create paper flowers by hand. Your box should be long and wide enough to carry or store your flower(s). The exact size is not important. It just needs to be large enough to keep your project and flower building tools secure. I started with my athletic shoe box then I bought a smaller one. Small paper boxes can be found at arts and crafts stores for less than two dollars at the time of this printing. Plastic food containers can also be used to store your project and tools needed too create paper flowers.

**Small Box**

# Wet napkin, wet towel or sponge #3

While creating your paper flowers, you will find it very useful to have a way to keep your fingers wet other then licking them. I like the cloth towel best that's my personal favorite. However a wet paper napkin or even a sponge will work just as well for keeping your fingers moist while perfecting your craft.

 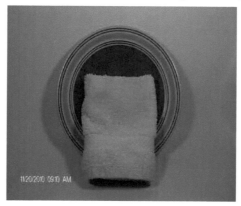 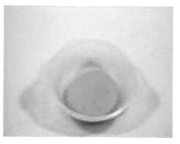

**Wet napkin**          **Wet towel**          **Wet sponge**

# Pencil or Pen #4

Use your pencil or pen to trace your pattern if needed. Also you can use your pen or pencil to punch holes in the bottom of your cup and turn it into an instant flower holder.

**Pencil**

**Pen**

# Paper cup or Foam Cup #5

Use you paper or foam cup to store your parts. Turn your cup upside down, punch very small holes, now you have an instant flower holder.

**Foam Cup**

**Paper Cup**

# Before we get started

The materials and techniques mentioned here are set up so that you can easily make a one leaf one petal flower within the next twenty minutes. Make sure the napkins is one ply. You can use two, or even four plies but remember the sheets will need to be separated. Separating napkins can be very time consuming and frustrating. The easiest thing to do is just use single ply napkins. At this time I'll introduce my helpful hints [brackets]. You'll see this when you get to areas where my patience and due diligence paid off. I'll save you the headache and share my secrets. The rules are very simple. tear from a single ply square napkin, roll all exposed edges, wrap together remaining material without any left over.

[Helpful Hints] A. Always start with a fresh napkin, no wrinkles.
                B. Edge with the single fold is along the top.
                C. The double single fold should be on your left side.

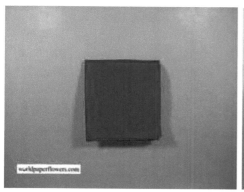
**1 (Square napkin)**

**2 (Separated Layers)**

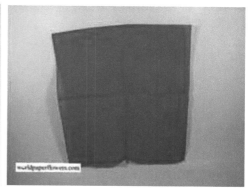
**3 (Preparation for tearing)**

**4 (From left to right)**

**5 (Top to bottom)**

**6 (Separate corner sheets)**

1 (Square napkin) Use a square napkin. You can use a horizontal napkin but you will need to do a re fold and tear it to make it square.

2 (Separate layers) If the napkin is two plies or multiple layers you must first separate before you proceed.

3 (Preparation for tearing) Places single ply square napkin flat on clean service.

4 (From left to right) keep napkin flat, fold and creases, from left to right.

5 (Top to bottom) Keep napkin flat, fold and crease, from top to bottom.

6 (Separate corner sheets) You should see four separate corner sheets on the right bottom corners. You have just prepared your napkin for tearing.

# Making a one pedal one leaf with stem paper flower

[Helpful Hints]
A. For things you must do for every flower 1. Have a pattern 2. Tear 3. Roll 4. wrap
B. Be patient and slow at first your speed will come with practice.
C. Always complete one task before you start the next.

Create your pattern before you can tear, you must first have a pattern to follow. Your next fold and creases will create that pattern there fore, press hard so that you can see your creases.

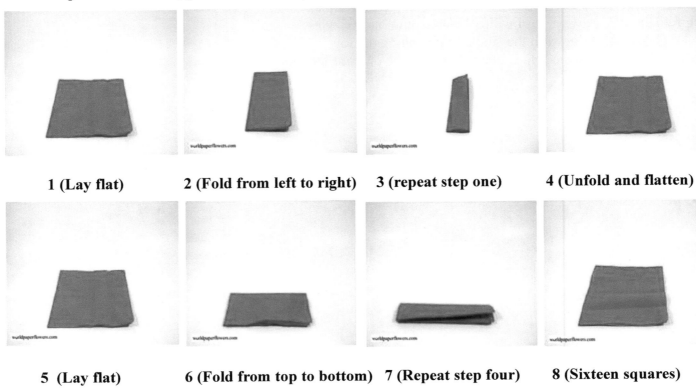

**1 (Lay flat)**     **2 (Fold from left to right)**     **3 (repeat step one)**     **4 (Unfold and flatten)**

**5 (Lay flat)**     **6 (Fold from top to bottom)**     **7 (Repeat step four)**     **8 (Sixteen squares)**

1 (Lay flat) Double check all corners for alignment before folding your napkin.
2 (Fold from left to right) Fold from left to right fold and crease the napkin.
3 (Repeat steps one) Fold and crease the napkin one more time.
4 (Unfold and flatten) Unfold and double check all corners.
5 (lay flat) Double check all corners for alignment before folding.
6 (Fold from top to bottom) Fold from top to bottom and crease the napkin.
7 (Repeat steps four) Fold and crease the napkin one more time.
8 (Sixteen squares) Now you should have sixteen squares, four columns and four rolls.

# Making Your First Lose Tears

[Helpful Hints]
A. Your tear will determine the outlook of your flower.  Be concerned with the quality of your first tear.
B. Always tear with the grain of the tissue from top to bottom.
C. Use a pen or pencil and trim edges if necessary.

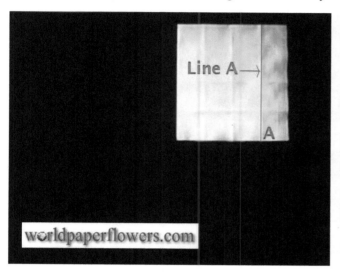

**1 (Tear crease A)**

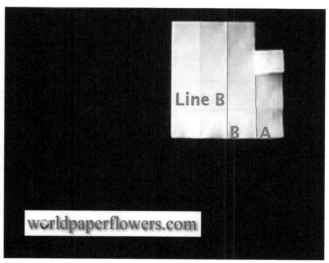

**2 (Tear Crease B)**

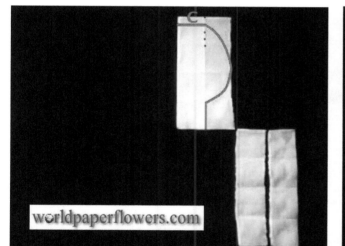

**3 (Tear line C1)**

**4 (Tea line C2)**

1 (Tear creases A) Tear along the crease (A) starting from the top to the bottom. At first go slow and use your fingers like scissors. Once you get the hang of it you'll be able to tear completely through the whole napkin in one quick motion. For now I suggest you go slow.

2 (Tear crease B) Tear along the crease

3 (Tear line C1) Section C will have two identical pieces. One of the pieces will be your petal the other will be used for your leaf. Keep your fingers close together using your finger nails like little scissors.

4 (Tear line C2) If you tear over the edge, it's okay just continue. Keep your tears neat and clean, be patient.

**5 (tear Line C3)**                     **6 (Tear Line C4)**

5 (Tear line C3) Continue tearing until you reach the bottom.

6 (tear Line C4) Once you complete tearing line C, place your remaining material below.

**7 (Place all torn material below)   8 (Tear line C5)        9 (Ready for rolling)**

7 (place all previously torn material below) Get in the habit of staying organized. When you get into more complicated flowers they will be easy to do if you learn good habits now.

8 (Tear line C5) When doing a cross grain tear, keep your fingers very close and tear a little at a time. Always start from the top and proceed to the bottom.

9 (Ready for rolling) your tearing for this flower is complete. Now it is time to get ready for rolling.

# How to Roll

[Helpful Hints]
A. Keep your napkin wrinkle free
B. Keep your fingers moist
C. Always pull tissue to the end before rolling

The main thing to remember while rolling your edges is to not over do it. Most tissue will allow you to handle it three maybe four times before it starts to fall apart. Try not to over water your fingers thinking they will stay moist longer. What will happen is you will ruin your napkin because your fingers are too wet.

**1 (Moist Fingers)**

**2 (Always start from bottom)**

**3 (First roll sets the tissue)**

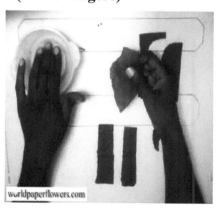

**4 (Stop at the top)**

**5 (Repeat process)**

**6 (Shape edges)**

1 (Moist finger) It's easy to roll petals and leafs with moist fingers. It's also very easy to separate closed petals and leafs with moist fingers.

2 (Always start from the bottom) Start from the bottom and work your way up.

3 (First roll sets the tissue) Always pulls edges of paper to the end before rolling.

4 (Stop at the top) Try to get a perfect point later, it will come with practice. Keep in mind you can only roll it so many times before it is ruined.

5 (Repeats process) Repeats process on other side starting from the bottom up. Don't forget to moist your finger tip.

6 (Shape edges) After doing our initial roll, then shape your petal or leaf so that it has an even edge.

# How to wrap

[Helpful Hints]
A. Keep your wrap wrinkle free
B. Try using different colors for your wrap.
C. Always keep your wrap as tight as possible.

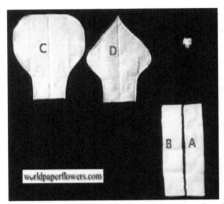
**1 (Preparation before wrapping)**

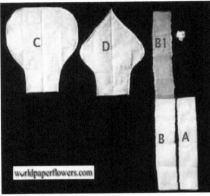
**2 (B1 to D and B2 C)**

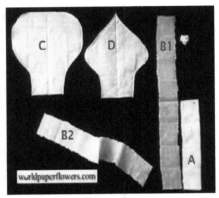
**3 (B1 to D and B2 to C)**

1 (Preparation before wrapping) Once you have rolled your petal and leaf you are ready to start wrapping.

2 (B1 to D and B2 to C) Takes wrap B2 and start wrapping C from the bottom until you run out.

3 (B1 to D and B2 to c) Takes wrap b1 and start wrapping D from the bottom until you run out.

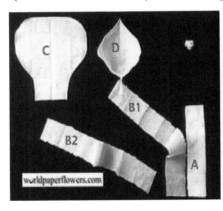
**4 (B1 to D and B2 to C)**

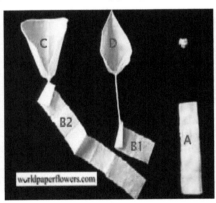
**5 (B1 to D B2 to C)**

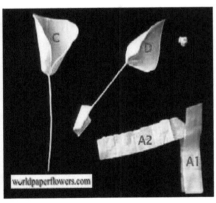
**6 (A2 to C/D)**

4 (B1 to D and B2 to C) Completely wrap B2 to C and B1 to D

5 (B1 to D and B2 to C) Completely wrap B2 to C and B1 to D

6 (A2 to C/D) Combine stem from D and C and wrap with A2 until you run out.

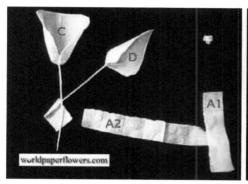
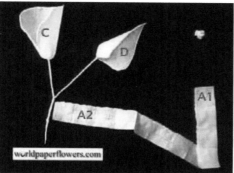
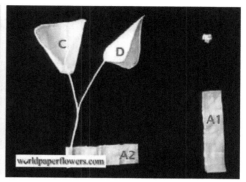

**7 (A2`to C/D)**        **8 (A2 to C/D)**        **9 (A2 to C/D)**

7 (A2 to C/D) Combine stem from D and C a wrap with A2 until you run out.
8 (A2 to C/D) Keep your wrapping as tight as possible. Don't make it too tight. It might break.
9 (A2 to C/D) While completing your wrap try to keep the stem as straight as possible.

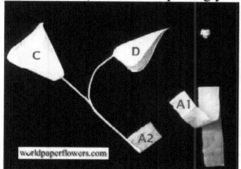
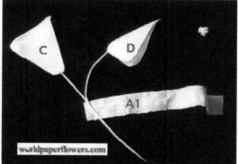
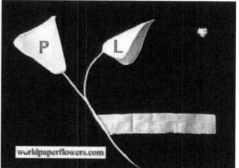

**10 (A2 to C/D)**        **11 (A1 to C/D)**        **12 (A2 to C/D)**

10 (A2 to C/D) Complete wrapping.
11 (A1 to C/D) again keep your wrapping as tight as possible. Start from the top and work your way down.
12 (A1 to C/D) Continue wrapping but at the very end moist your fingers and roll your stem tight to lock in your wrap.

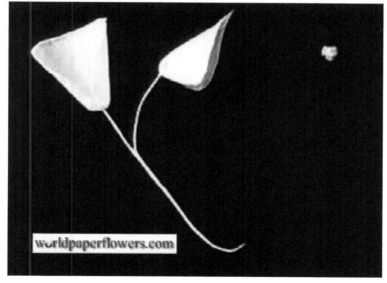

**Congratulations you are done.**

# How to read a pattern

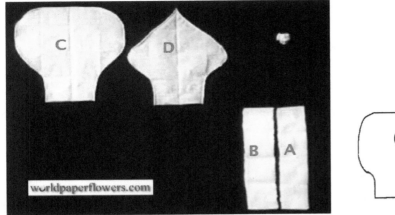 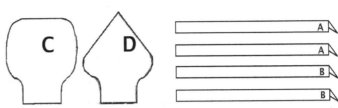

For the sake of keeping it simple all free instructions patterns are labeled a, b, c, d,. I also used one complete wrap for each wrapping instead of tearing them into sections. There will be couple of minor changes made here in the book to keep it simple. Instead of having a, b, c, d to identify the parts you will have P, L, W, S, To or P=petals, L=Leafs, W=wraps, S=Style, T=Trash, when you get into more complex flowers this will make it easier for me to guide you through.

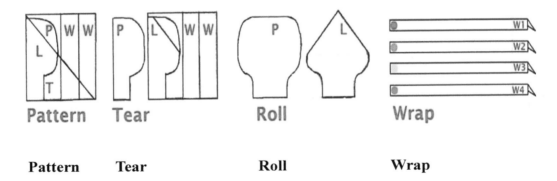

| Pattern | Tear | Roll | Wrap |
| --- | --- | --- | --- |

**Pattern**     **Tear**          **Roll**          **Wrap**

You will notice on the bottom of every pattern you will see pattern, tear, roll, and wrap. Each step is broke down so that you can see how the napkin is laid out before the tears begin. You will also be able to see folds before you tear the napkin. the next step is rolling. just remember the basic rules (roll all outside exposed edges). Last but not least is wrapping. The reason I fold my wrapping is it leaves a very clean line and it makes the tissue twice as strong there fore you can apply more tension while wrapping. Which in return will give you a tighter and more rigid stem or whatever you may be wrapping at that time.

I'll skip the sections on how to tear, roll and wrap from this point. When I need for you to perform one of these tasks, I will indicate that task by just writing tear, roll or wrap.

The flowers are grouped together in three different categories. One through three is the beginner level. Four through seven is the medium level, with the introduction of the center piece or style. At first the style will be labeled T for trash but will eventually become S for style. Eight through eleven are the advanced levels and twelve is a creation from you. That is why it's called a miracle flower it was a gift from god to you now you can share it with others.

Love

Courage

Adventure

**This is the beginner level.**

Family

Forgiveness

Hope and Faith

Freedom and Prosperity

**This is the medium level.**

Health and Wellness

Protection

Appreciation

Comforting A
Grieving Heart

Miracle

**This is the advanced level.**

**Love**

**Pattern**

**Tear**

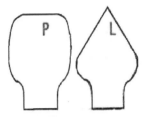

**Roll**

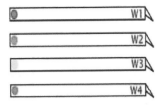

**Wrap**

Wrapping Instructions [helpful Hints] A. Keep your fingers close while tearing.
B. Trim your edges if needed.
C. Keep petals and leafs wrinkle free.

## Steps
☐ Create pattern
☐ Tear
☐ Roll
☐ Wrap

**(Inventory Check)**

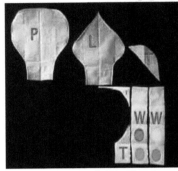

P=Petal, L=Leaf, T=Trash
(Wrap = 1,2,3,4)

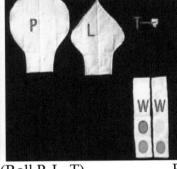

(Roll P, L, T)
(Roll up T=Trash)

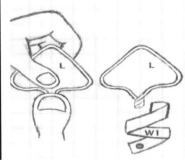

Prep L (twist bottom)
(Wrap = 1,2,3,4)(L to W1) red

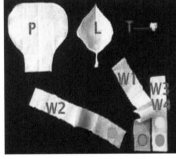

(Separate wrap W1&W2)

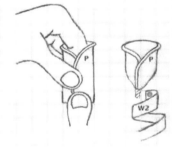

Prep P (Insert finger twist bottom)
(P to w2) Orange Wrap

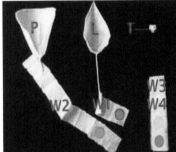

Prep P, Wrap P
(P to W2) orange wrap

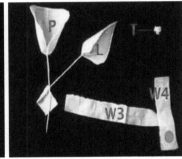

(Prep connection using leaf wrap)
(P/L to W3) Yellow wrap

(Squeeze tight while wrapping (P/L to W3)
Yellow Wrap

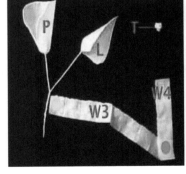

(Keep stem straight for Wrapping)
(P/L W3) yellow Wrap

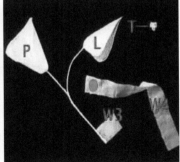

Moist fingers before last wrap
(P/L, W3 to W4) Green wrap

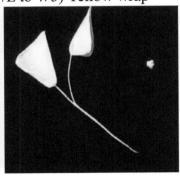

(Congratulations you are done).

Courage

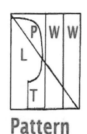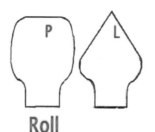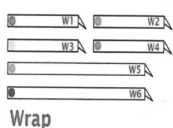

**Pattern**  **Tear**  **Roll**  **Wrap**

**Courage**　　**Pattern**　**Tear**　　　**Roll**　　**Wrap**

Wrapping instructions [Helpful Hints] A. keep your fingers close while tearing.
B. Trim your edges if needed
C. Keep petals and leafs wrinkle free.

# Steps
☐ **Create pattern**
☐ **Tear**
☐ **Roll**
☐ **Wrap**

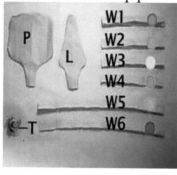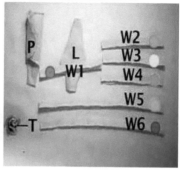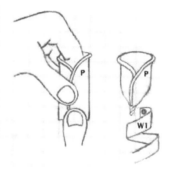

(Inventory Check)　　P-Petal, L-Leaf, T-Trash　　(Roll P, L, T)　　　Prep P (Insert finger
Wrap = 1,2,3,4,5,6　　(Roll up trash)　Twist bottom) (P to W1) Red

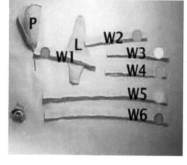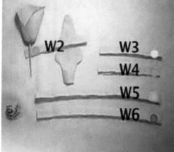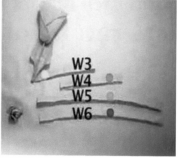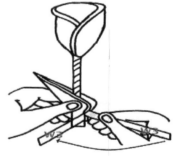

Keep your petal in position　Use W2 for your second wrap　Prep L　　(keep petal and leaf in the same)
(P to W1) Red　　(P, W1, to W2) Orange　(P/L to W3)　direction) (W3 between P Stem)
Yellow

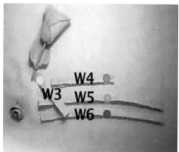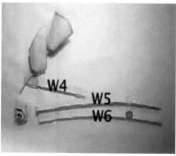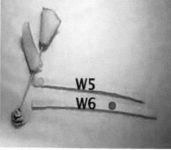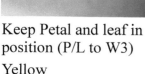

Keep Petal and leaf in　Use W4 your next wrap　Use W5 for your next wrap Use W6 for your next wrap
position (P/L to W3)　(P/L, W3 to W4)　(P/L, W3,W4 to W5)　(P/L, W3,W4,W5 to W6)
Yellow　　　　Green　　　　Lt. Blue　　　　Blue

**(Moisten fingers before last wrap)**
**Congratulations you are done!**

Adventure

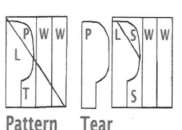 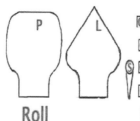  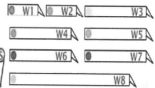

Pattern  Tear  Style  Roll  Wrap

**Adventure**  **Pattern**  **Tear**  **Style**  **Roll**  **Wrap**

Wrapping instructions [Helpful Hints] A. keep your fingers close while tearing.
B. Trim your edges if needed
C. Keep petals and leafs wrinkle free.

## Steps
☐ **Create pattern**
☐ **Tear**
☐ **Roll**
☐ **Wrap**

(Inventory Check)

P-Petal, L-Leaf, S-style
Wrap – 1,2,3,4,5,6,7,8

Always prep Style first
(Use S parts to create style)

Squeeze hard while forming
Style (Prep style)

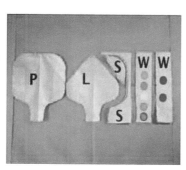 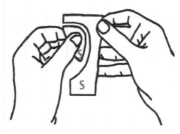 

Leave small stem for Style
stem)

Inventory check P, L, S, W 1-8

(Tear W1) Wrap style
using W1 (S to W) Red

(Roll W1 leaving small
(S to W1) Red

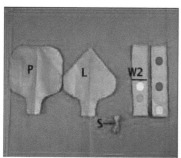 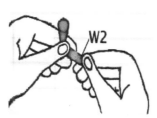 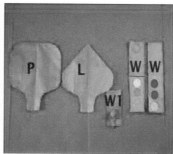 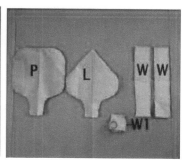

Prep S before wrapping

(S, W1 to W2)
(S to W2) Orange

(Wrap using W2)
(S to W2) Orange

(Inventory Check)
P, L, S, W 3-8

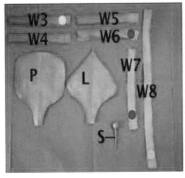 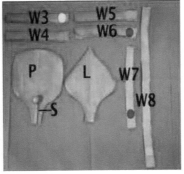 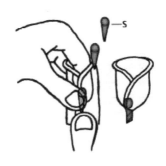 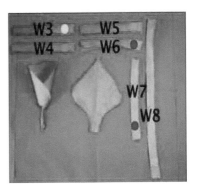

(Roll P-Petal, L-Leaf)    (Prep Style on Petal)   (Prep Style in Petal and twist)(Inventory check P, L, W 3-8)

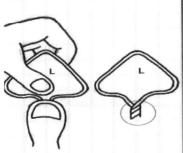 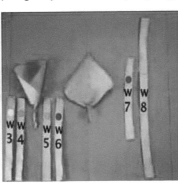 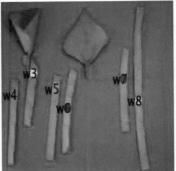 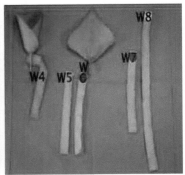

(Prep Leaf twist bottom) (Inventory check) P, L, W 3-8 (Prep W3)          (Prep W4)
                                              (P to W3) Yellow wrap   (P, W3 to W4) Green Wrap

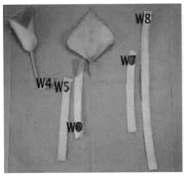 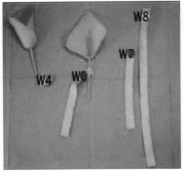 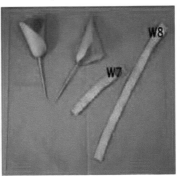 

(Prep W5)               (Prep W6)              (Combine Petal and Leaf)  (Prep W7)
(L to W5) Lt. Blue      (L, W5 to W6) Blue     (Prep P/L)               (P/L to W7) Purple

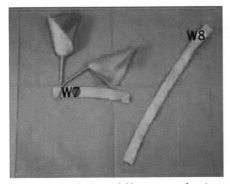 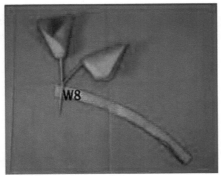 

(Squeeze tight while wrapping)   (Prep W8) (Moisten fingers)   (Congratulations Good Job! )
(P/L to W7) Purple               (P/L, W7 to W8) Pink

worldpaperflowers.com

**Family**

    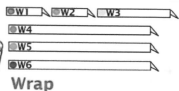

| Pattern | Tear | Style | Roll | Wrap |

**Family** **Pattern** **Tear** **Style** **Roll** **Wrap**

Wrapping instructions [Helpful Hints] A. keep Petal and leafs wrinkle free.
B. Roll your Petals and Leafs even from beginning to end. C. Prep or twist the bottoms of your Petal(s) or Leaf(s) this will help them stay in position while wrapping.

## Steps
☐ Create pattern
☐ Tear
☐ Roll
☐ Wrap

(Inventory Check)

P-Petal, L-Leaf, S-Style
Wrap – 1,2,3,4,5,6)

Always prep Style first
Use S parts to create Style)

Squeeze hard while forming
Style (Prep Style)

(Roll Style into hard round
ball) (Prep Style)

(Tear W1) (tear W2)
(S to W1) Red wrap

(Roll Style with W1 form small
stem) (S to W1) Red wrap

Roll Style leaving small
(S to W1) Red wrap

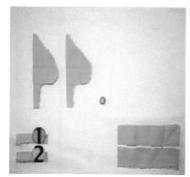   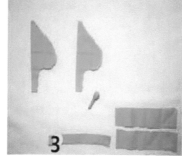 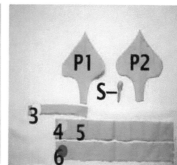 

Prep S before wrapping

(wrap using W2)
(S, W1 to W2) Orange wrap

(Roll P1, P2)

(Inventory Check)
P1,2 S, W 3-6

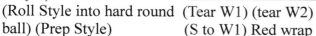

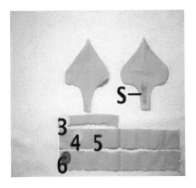

(Roll P 1, 2)

(Prep S on P and twist)

(Prep S in P and twist)

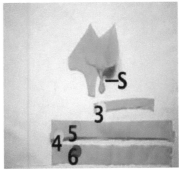

(Inventory Check P, L, W 3-6)

(Keep Petals in opposite directions) (W3 between P1 & p2 Yellow wraps

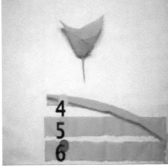

(Inventory Check) P1,2 W4-6

(Prep W4)
(P to W4) Green wrap

(Prep W5)
(P, W4 to W5)Lt. Blue Wrap

Use W6 for your next wrap
(P, W4,6 to W6) Blue Wrap

Moist fingers for last wrap
Congratulations you are done!

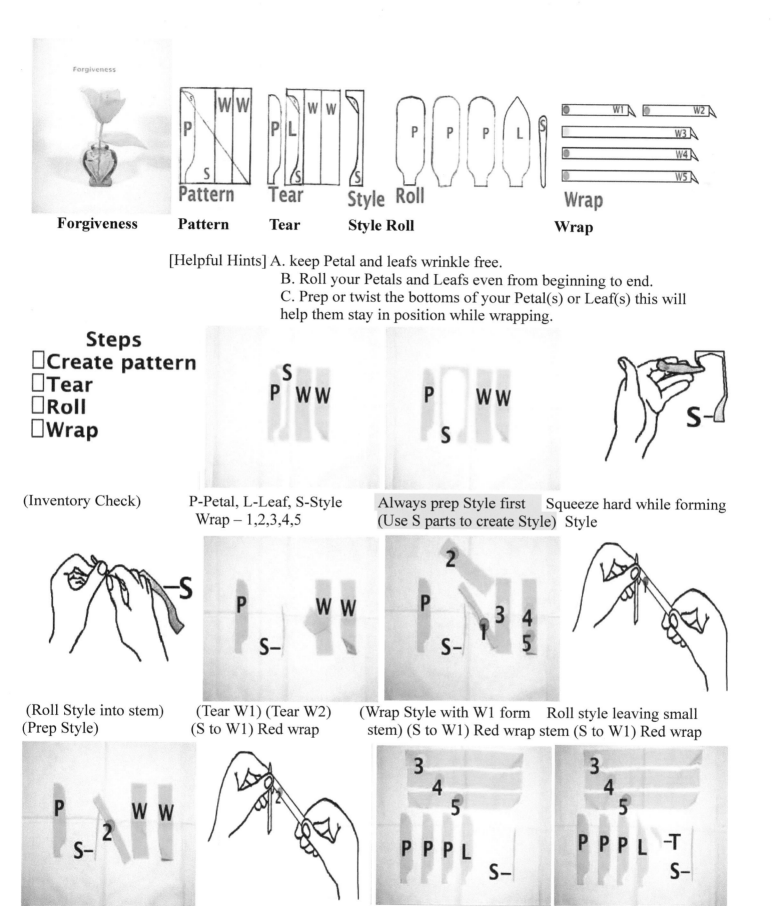

Forgiveness

Pattern | Tear | Style Roll | Wrap

[Helpful Hints] A. keep Petal and leafs wrinkle free.
B. Roll your Petals and Leafs even from beginning to end.
C. Prep or twist the bottoms of your Petal(s) or Leaf(s) this will help them stay in position while wrapping.

## Steps
☐ Create pattern
☐ Tear
☐ Roll
☐ Wrap

(Inventory Check)

P-Petal, L-Leaf, S-Style
Wrap – 1,2,3,4,5

Always prep Style first
(Use S parts to create Style)   Squeeze hard while forming Style

(Roll Style into stem)
(Prep Style)

(Tear W1) (Tear W2)
(S to W1) Red wrap

(Wrap Style with W1 form stem) (S to W1) Red wrap stem   Roll style leaving small stem (S to W1) Red wrap

Prep S before wrapping
(S, W1 to W2)

(Wrap using W2)
(S to W2)  Orange wrap

(Separate P1,2,3 and L)
(Prep L)

(Tear L into Leaf shape)

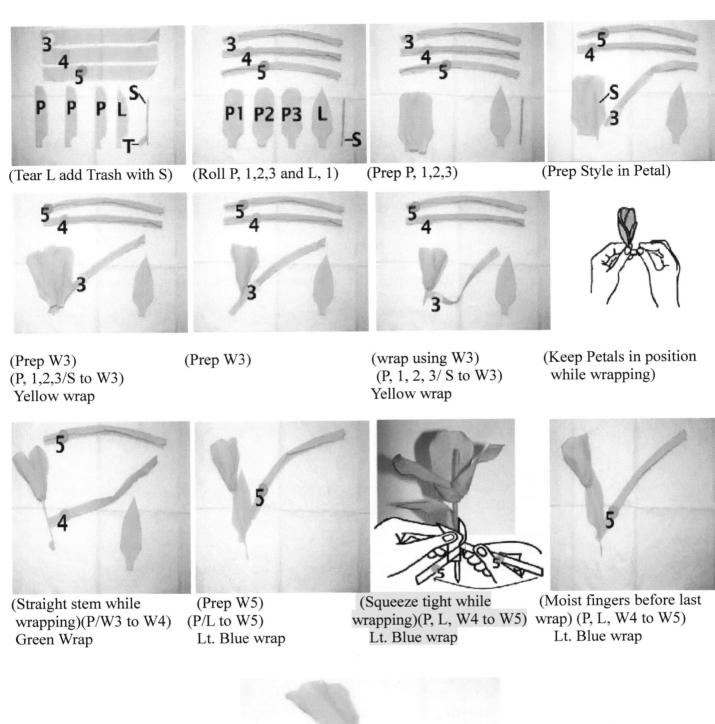

(Tear L add Trash with S)

(Roll P, 1,2,3 and L, 1)

(Prep P, 1,2,3)

(Prep Style in Petal)

(Prep W3)
(P, 1,2,3/S to W3)
Yellow wrap

(Prep W3)

(wrap using W3)
(P, 1, 2, 3/ S to W3)
Yellow wrap

(Keep Petals in position
while wrapping)

(Straight stem while
wrapping)(P/W3 to W4)
Green Wrap

(Prep W5)
(P/L to W5)
Lt. Blue wrap

(Squeeze tight while
wrapping)(P, L, W4 to W5)
Lt. Blue wrap

(Moist fingers before last
wrap) (P, L, W4 to W5)
Lt. Blue wrap

**Congratulations you are done!**

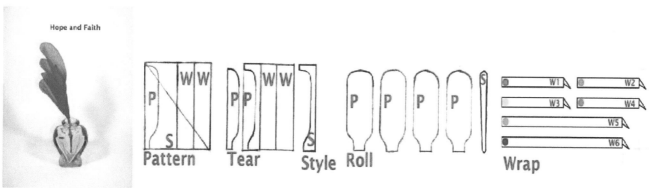

**Hope and Faith**     **Pattern**     **Tear**     **Style**   **Roll**       **Wrap**

Wrapping instructions [Helpful Hints] A. keep Petal and leafs wrinkle free.

B. Roll your Petals and Leafs even from beginning to end.

C. Prep or twist the bottoms of your Petal(s) or Leaf(s) this will help them stay in position while wrapping

**Steps**
- ☐ Create pattern
- ☐ Tear
- ☐ Roll
- ☐ Wrap

(Inventory Check)     P-Petal, S-Style,        (Always prep Style first)   Squeeze hard while forming

(Wrap – 1,2,3,4,5,6      Use S parts to create Style)   Style (Prep Style)

(Roll Style into stem) (Tear W1) (Tear W2)(Roll Style with W1 form small (Roll Style leaving small stem) Prep
Style)       (S to W1) Red wrap       stem) (S to w1) Red wrap (S to W1) Red wrap

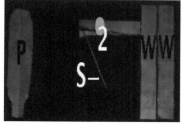 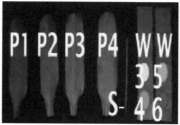 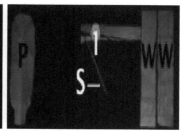 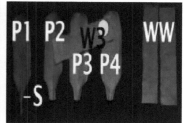

Prep S before wrapping     (Wrap using W2)     (Roll P1 P2, P3, P4)     (Inventory Check)

(S, W1 to W2)       (S to W2) Orange wrap         (P1,2,3,4/ S/ W 3-6)

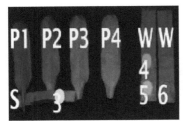  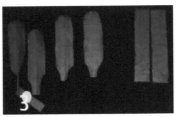 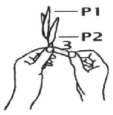

(Prep W3)          (Prep S on P and twist bottom)   (Prep S in P1 and wrap)    Keep Petals in same direction
                                                    (P/S to W3) Yellow

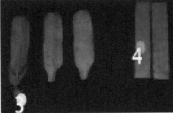 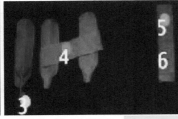 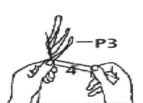 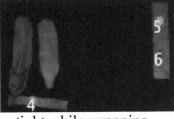

(Tear W4)              (Prep W4) (fold W4) (Keep Petals in same direction)Squeeze tight while wrapping
                                           (P1,2,3 to W4) Green wrap   (P1,2,3,to W4) Green wrap

  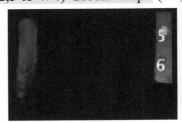 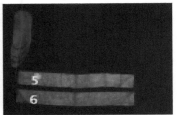

(Keep using W4 to finish)      (Keep petals in the same direction)    (Prep W5, W6)      (Fold W5,W6)
(P1,2,3,4 to W4) Green wrap(Squeeze tight while wrapping)

  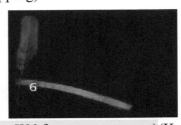 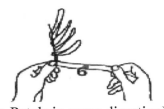

(Prep W5)          (Keep Petals in same direction) (Use W6 for our next wrap)(Keep Petals in same direction)
                   (P to W5) Lt. Blue Wrap         (Straight stem while wrapping) (P to W6) Blue wrap

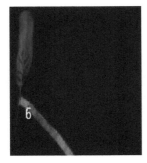 

(Moisten fingers before last wrap)    (Congratulations you are done! )
(P to W6) Blue wrap

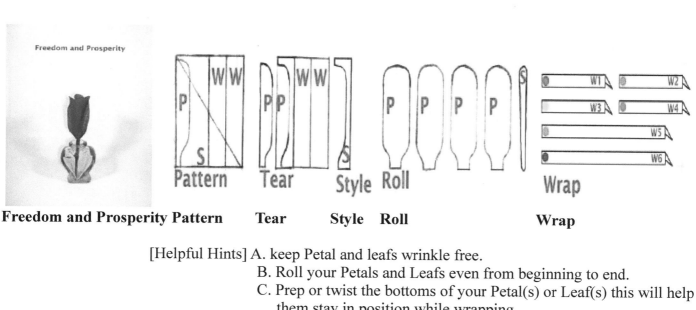

Freedom and Prosperity

**Freedom and Prosperity Pattern**  **Tear**  **Style**  **Roll**  **Wrap**

[Helpful Hints] A. keep Petal and leafs wrinkle free.
B. Roll your Petals and Leafs even from beginning to end.
C. Prep or twist the bottoms of your Petal(s) or Leaf(s) this will help them stay in position while wrapping.

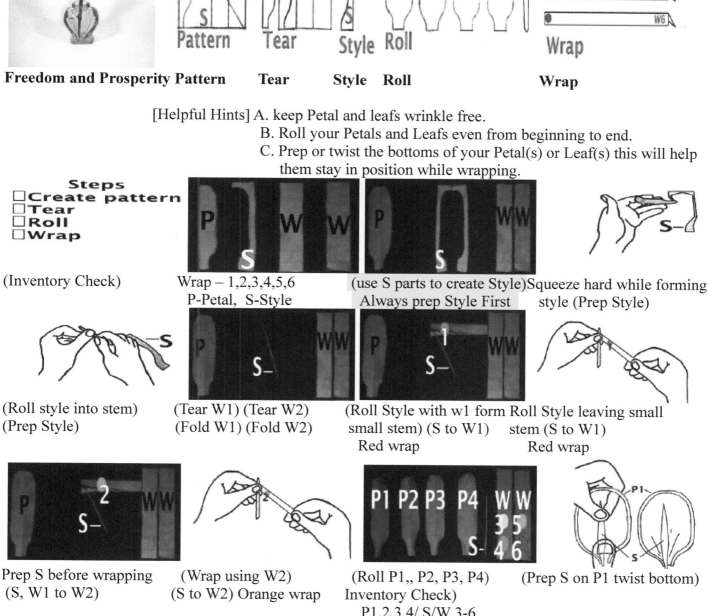

**Steps**
☐ Create pattern
☐ Tear
☐ Roll
☐ Wrap

(Inventory Check)

Wrap – 1,2,3,4,5,6
P-Petal, S-Style

(use S parts to create Style)
Always prep Style First

Squeeze hard while forming style (Prep Style)

(Roll style into stem)
(Prep Style)

(Tear W1) (Tear W2)
(Fold W1) (Fold W2)

(Roll Style with w1 form small stem) (S to W1)
Red wrap

Roll Style leaving small stem (S to W1)
Red wrap

Prep S before wrapping
(S, W1 to W2)

(Wrap using W2)
(S to W2) Orange wrap

(Roll P1,, P2, P3, P4)
Inventory Check)
P1,2,3,4/ S/W 3-6

(Prep S on P1 twist bottom)

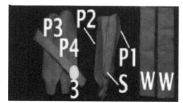

Prep S in P1 to P2 (tear w3)
P1, L/P2 to W3)
Yellow wrap

Keep Petals in opposite direction (P1, L/ P2 to W3)
Yellow wrap

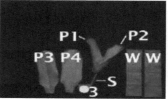

(Inventory check)
P3, 4/ W4,5,6

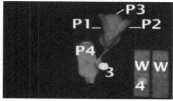

(Prep P3 and P4 twist bottom)

 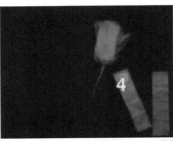  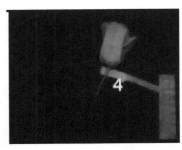

(Squeeze tight while wrapping)      (Prep W4) (Fold W4)      (Keeping Petals in position while wrapping) Green wrap      (Keep stem straight while wrapping) (P to W4) Green wrap

 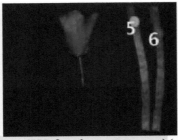 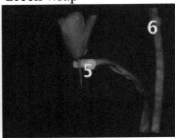 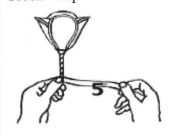

(Inventory Check) (P/ W5,6)      (Use W5 for the next wrap)(prep W5,W6)(Fold W5, W6) (P, W4 to W5) Lt. Blue      (Straight stem while wrapping)(P, W4 to W5) Lt. Blue

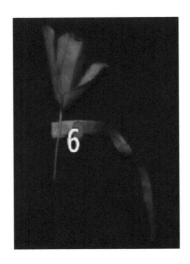 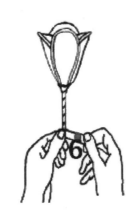 

(Use W6 for your next wrap) (P, W5 to W6) Blue wrap      Moist fingers before last wrap (P, W5 to W6) Blue wrap      Congratulations you are done!

**Health and Wellness**

**Pattern**

**Tear**

**Style Roll**

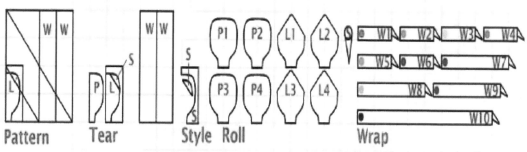

**Wrap**

**Pattern    Tear      Style Roll              Wrap**

[Helpful Hints] A. Prep or twist the bottoms of your Petal(s) or Leaf(s) this will help them stay in position while wrapping.
B. Always fold your wrapping.
C. Always wet your fingers for last wrap.

## Steps
- ☐ **Create pattern**
- ☐ **Tear**
- ☐ **Roll**
- ☐ **Wrap**

(Inventory Check)

(Fold down left side of napkin)

(Fold from left to right) (Squeeze or press your fold)

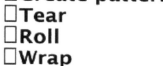

(Tear your pattern)

(Separated your 4 Petals and 4 Leafs)

(Tear your Leafs)

(Always prep Style First)
(Use S parts to create Style)

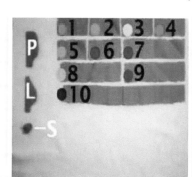

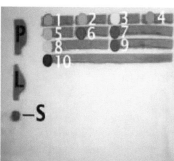

(Squeeze hard while forming Style)

(Roll your Style into a tight ball)

(Tear your wraps)

(Inventory Check)
(1,2,3,4/L 1,2,3,4/ S /W 1-10)
(Fold all ten wraps)

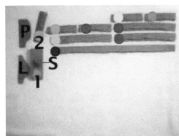
(Roll Style using W1)
(S to W1) Red w rap

(Roll W1 forming small stem)(twist the bottom of style)

Use W2 for your next wrap

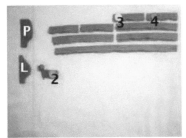
(Wrap using W2)
(S/ W1 to W2) orange wrap

(Moist fingers for next wrap)(Squeeze tight while wrapping)

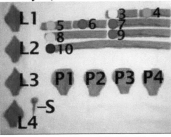
(Inventory Check) Roll P 1-4/L1-4)(P1,2,3,4/s/w1-10

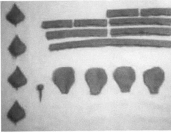
(prep all leaf bottoms)

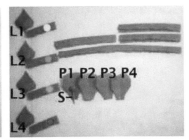
Prep all wraps

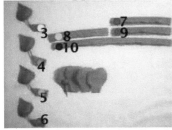
Wrap using w3,w4,w5,w6 (L1-w3/L2-w4/L3-W5/ L4-W6

(Overlap Petals prep S in middle) (Squeeze tight while wrapping)

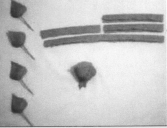
Keep Petals in position while preparing for wrap.

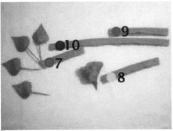
(Use W7 for next wrap)
(L 1-3, 4 to W7)
Purple wrap

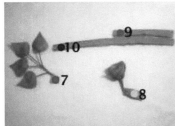
Half way through W7 add L4 (P1-4 to W8)
Pink wrap

(Combine Petals and leafs) (P 1-4/ l 1-4 to W9) Brown

Keep the Petal stem as straight as possible while wrapping

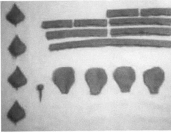
Use W10 for next wrapping (P1-4/ L1-4/W9 to W10)
Green wrap

(Moisten fingers last wrap)

(Congratulation you are done!

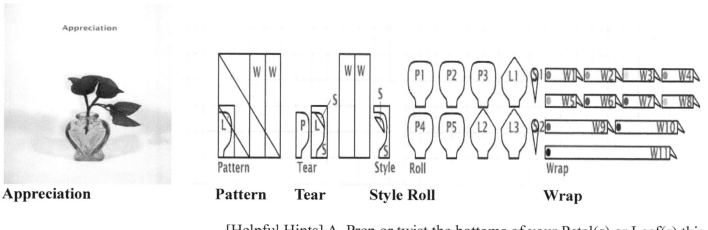

**Appreciation**　　　　　**Pattern**　　**Tear**　　**Style Roll**　　　　**Wrap**

[Helpful Hints] A. Prep or twist the bottoms of your Petal(s) or Leaf(s) this
will help them stay in position while wrapping.
B. Always fold your wrapping.
C. Always wet your fingers for last wrap.

## Steps
☐ **Create pattern**
☐ **Tear**
☐ **Roll**
☐ **Wrap**

(Inventory Check)

(Tear Line A and Line B)　(Fold down left side of napkin)　(Fold from left to right)

(Tear your pattern)

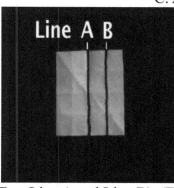

Separate 5 Petals and 3 leafs

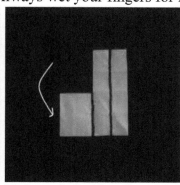

(Tear Leaf pattern)

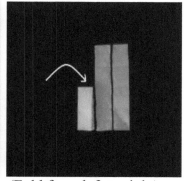

(Tear in the middle of S)

Roll two separate balls
with S

(Squeeze S1, S2 tight while
forming)

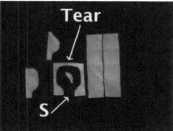

(Use the Leaf tear to wrap
your balls)

(Squeeze tight while
forming balls)

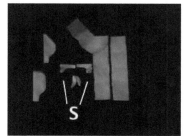

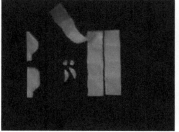

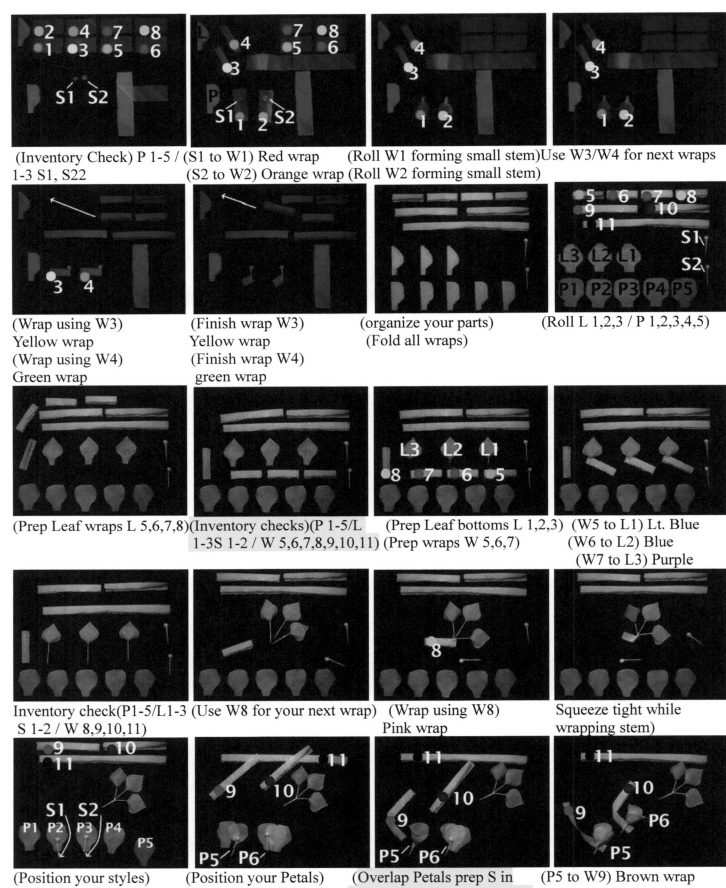

(Inventory Check) P 1-5 / (S1 to W1) Red wrap (Roll W1 forming small stem) Use W3/W4 for next wraps
1-3 S1, S22 (S2 to W2) Orange wrap (Roll W2 forming small stem)

(Wrap using W3) (Finish wrap W3) (organize your parts) (Roll L 1,2,3 / P 1,2,3,4,5)
Yellow wrap Yellow wrap (Fold all wraps)
(Wrap using W4) (Finish wrap W4)
Green wrap green wrap

(Prep Leaf wraps L 5,6,7,8) (Inventory checks)(P 1-5/L (Prep Leaf bottoms L 1,2,3) (W5 to L1) Lt. Blue
1-3S 1-2 / W 5,6,7,8,9,10,11) (Prep wraps W 5,6,7) (W6 to L2) Blue
(W7 to L3) Purple

Inventory check(P1-5/L1-3 (Use W8 for your next wrap) (Wrap using W8) Squeeze tight while
S 1-2 / W 8,9,10,11) Pink wrap wrapping stem)

(Position your styles) (Position your Petals) (Overlap Petals prep S in (P5 to W9) Brown wrap
(Position S1 to P2) (P1, P2 to S1) middle)(Squeeze tight while (P6 to W10) Green wrap
(Position S2 to P3) (P3,P4,P5 to S2) wrapping)

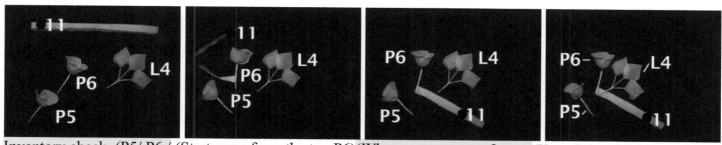

Inventory check  (P5/ P6 /   (Start wrap from the top P6)(When you run out of stem (Keep L4 and P5 in position
L4 / W11)                          (Use W11) Black wrap      L4 and P5 on opposite sides)   add while wrapping)

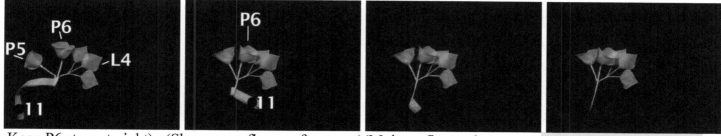

  Keep P6 stem straight)   (Shape your flower after wrap)(Moisten fingers last wrap) Congratulations you are
                                                                                           done!

Miracle Flower #1

Miracle Flower #2

Miracle Flower #3

Miracle Flower #4

Miracle Flower #5

Miracle Flower #6

Miracle Flower #7

Miracle Flower #8

Miracle Flower #9

Miracle Flower #10

Miracle Flower #11

Miracle Flower #12

# Coming Soon Book Two

**Protection**

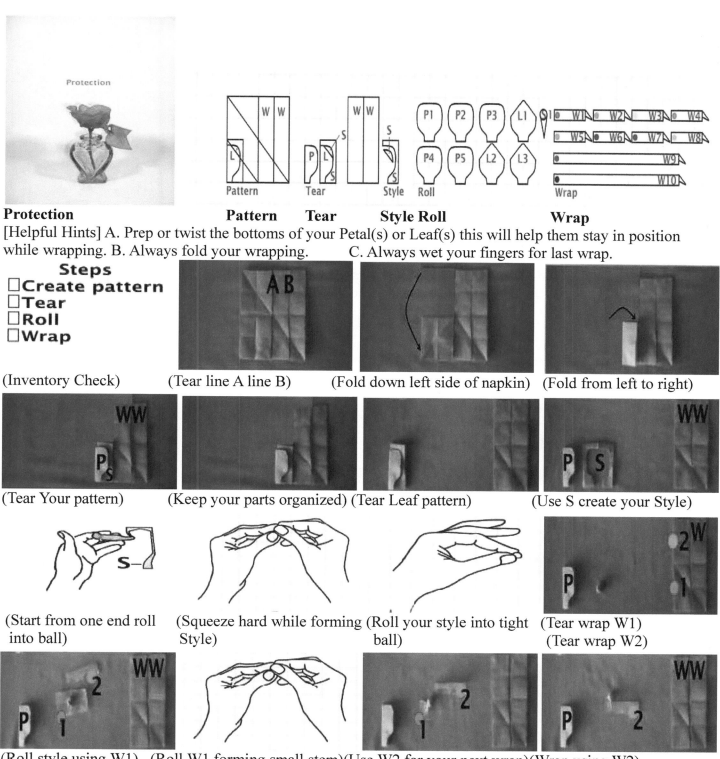

**Pattern** **Tear** **Style Roll** **Wrap**

[Helpful Hints] A. Prep or twist the bottoms of your Petal(s) or Leaf(s) this will help them stay in position while wrapping. B. Always fold your wrapping. C. Always wet your fingers for last wrap.

## Steps
☐ **Create pattern**
☐ **Tear**
☐ **Roll**
☐ **Wrap**

(Inventory Check)

(Tear line A line B)

(Fold down left side of napkin)

(Fold from left to right)

(Tear Your pattern)

(Keep your parts organized)

(Tear Leaf pattern)

(Use S create your Style)

(Start from one end roll into ball)

(Squeeze hard while forming Style)

(Roll your style into tight ball)

(Tear wrap W1)
(Tear wrap W2)

(Roll style using W1)

(Roll W1 forming small stem)
(twist the bottom of the style)

(Use W2 for your next wrap)

(Wrap using W2)
(S/W1 to W2) Orange wrap

(Moist fingers for next wrap) Squeeze tight while wrapping.

(separate 5 petals and 3 Leafs)

(Tear Leaf Pattern)

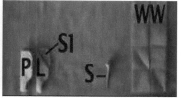

Store Leaf
(Tear S1 next to wraps)

  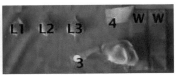 

(Separate Petals and Leafs) (Inventory Check) L1-3 (Roll L 1-3 / P 1-5) (Prep Leaf bottoms L 1-3)
/ P 1-5 / S / S1 / W 3-10 (Prep Petal bottoms P 1-5)

 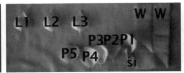 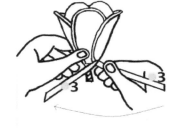

(Inventory Check) L 1-3 / (Overlap Petals 1-5) (Use W3 for your next wrap) (Wrap using W3)
(P 1-5 / S /S1 / W 3-10 (Prep S in middle of P1) (Squeeze tight while wrapping) (P 1-5 to W3)
Yellow wrap

  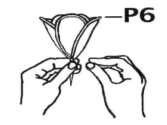 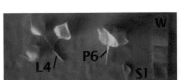

(Keep petals in position) (Use W4 for your next wrap) (Prep P6 twist bottom) (wrap using W8)
(Wet fingers for this wrap) (wrap using W4) Green wrap (wrap with moist fingers) (L1 / L2 / L3 / to W8)
Pink wrap

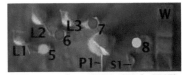  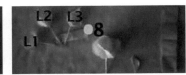 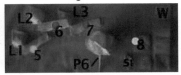

(Wrap using W5, W6, W7) (Lt. Blue W5 /Lt. Blue wrap) Use W8 for your next Wrap Prep (L1 to W5)
(L1 to W5) (L2 to W6) (Blue W6 / Blue wrap) (L2 to W6)
(L3 to W7) (Green W7 / Green wrap) (L3 to W7)

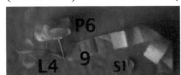 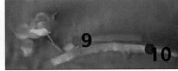  

(Combine Petals and Leafs) (Squeeze tight while (Keep P6 stem straight (Use W10 for next wrapping)
(P6 to W9) Brown wrap wrapping) possible while wrapping) (Prep S1 for wrapping)

(Position S1 at beginning of wrap) (Moisten fingers last wrap) (Congratulations you are done! )
(P6, L4, W9 to W0) Green wrap

**Comforting A Grieving Heart**

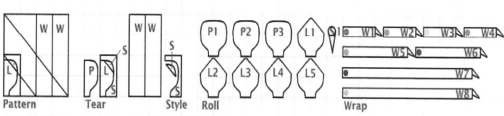

**Comforting A Grieving Heart Pattern**     **Tear**     **Style Roll**       **Wrap**

[Helpful Hints] A. Prep or twist the bottoms of your Petal(s) or Leaf(s) this will help them stay in position while wrapping. B. Always fold your wrapping.

C. Always wet your fingers for last wrap.

### Steps
- ☐ **Create pattern**
- ☐ **Tear**
- ☐ **Roll**
- ☐ **Wrap**

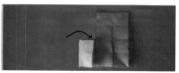

(Inventory Check)

(Tear Line A and Line B) (Fold down left side of napkin) (Fold from left to right)

(Tear your pattern)   (Keep your parts organized)(Trim your edges if needed) (Use S to create your Style)

(Start from one end roll into ball)   (Squeeze hard while forming style)   (Roll your style into tight ball)   (Tear wrap W1) (Tear wrap W2)

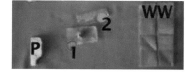   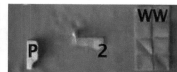

(Roll Style using W1) (S to W1) Red wrap   Roll W1 Forming small stem (twist the bottom of style)   (Use W2 for your next wrap)   (wrap using W2) (S / W1 to W2) Orange wrap

  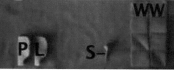 

(Moist fingers for next wrap squeeze tight while wrapping)   (Separate 5 Petals and 3 Leafs) (Tear Leaf pattern)   (Store Leaf tear S1 next to wraps)

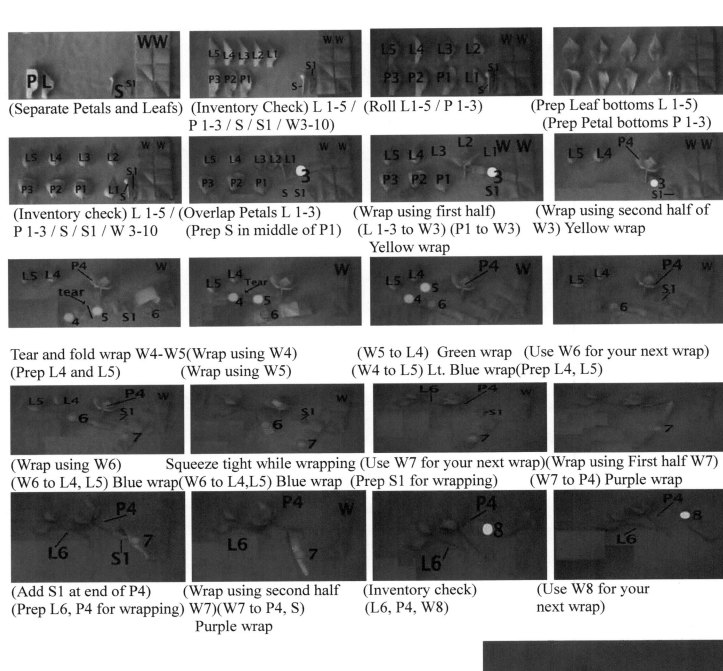

(Separate Petals and Leafs) (Inventory Check) L 1-5 / (Roll L1-5 / P 1-3) (Prep Leaf bottoms L 1-5)
P 1-3 / S / S1 / W3-10) (Prep Petal bottoms P 1-3)

(Inventory check) L 1-5 / (Overlap Petals L 1-3) (Wrap using first half) (Wrap using second half of
P 1-3 / S / S1 / W 3-10 (Prep S in middle of P1) (L 1-3 to W3) (P1 to W3) W3) Yellow wrap
Yellow wrap

Tear and fold wrap W4-W5 (Wrap using W4) (W5 to L4) Green wrap (Use W6 for your next wrap)
(Prep L4 and L5) (Wrap using W5) (W4 to L5) Lt. Blue wrap (Prep L4, L5)

(Wrap using W6) Squeeze tight while wrapping (Use W7 for your next wrap) (Wrap using First half W7)
(W6 to L4, L5) Blue wrap (W6 to L4,L5) Blue wrap (Prep S1 for wrapping) (W7 to P4) Purple wrap

(Add S1 at end of P4) (Wrap using second half (Inventory check) (Use W8 for your
(Prep L6, P4 for wrapping) W7)(W7 to P4, S) (L6, P4, W8) next wrap)
Purple wrap

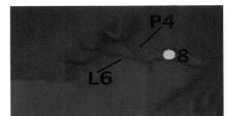

(wrap using W8)
(W8 to P4, L6) Pink wrap

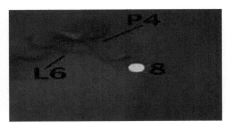

(Moisten fingers last wrap)

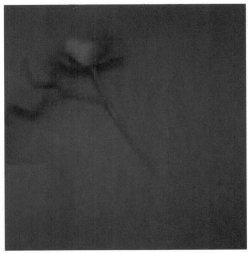

**Congratulations you are done!**

# How to make your own Tenon-Gami Flower Card

## General Supplies

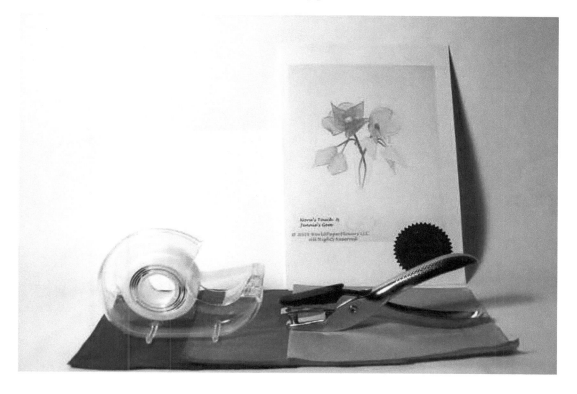

**1. Transparent tape**    **2. Hole puncher**    **3. New or Used card**

## Steps for making card.

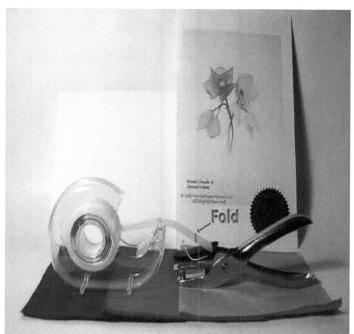

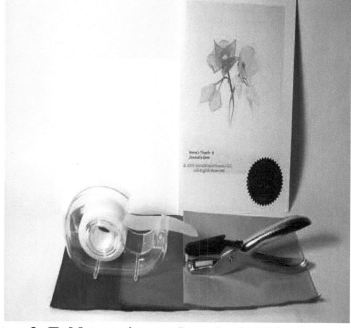

**Step 1. Pull transparent tape one an a half inch.**

**Step 2. Fold tape inward at the half inch and press hard.**

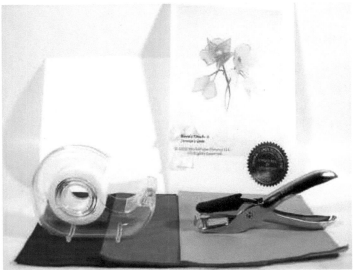
Step 3. Press or squeeze hard to remove air bubbles.

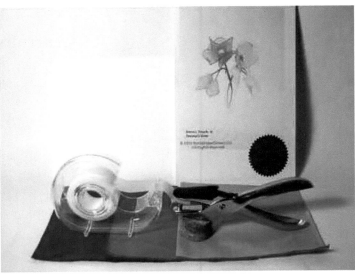
Step 4. Punch hole on folded side of tape.

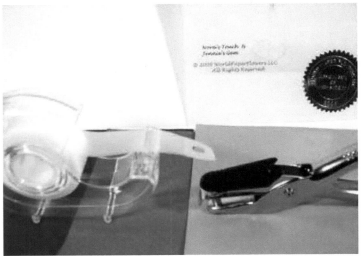
Step 5. Tear tape, place one half inch from left side, one inch from bottom.

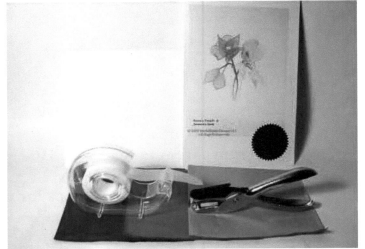
Step 6. Repeat steps 1-5, place second strip directly above step 5.

Step 7. Place flower stem through holes punched. (Use your old cards too! )

Step 8. Send your creation to family and friends with a personalized gold sealed box.

# Official Colors For Tenko-Gami

LOVE

COURAGE

ADVENTURE

FAMILY

FORGIVENESS

HOPE AND FAITH

FREEDOM AND PROSPERITY

HEALTH AND WELLNESS

APPRECIATION

PROTECTION

COMFORT A GRIEVING HEART

MIRACLE FLOWER

WORLD PAPER FLOWERS, LLC
OFFICIAL SEAL OF AUTHENTICITY
2009

# worldpaperflowers.com

# We Don't Fold, We Roll.

Love  Courage  Adventure  Family  Forgiveness

Hope & Faith

**Complete Instructions for Making Your Very Own**

## Paper Flowers  Book One

Freedom & Prosperity  Health & Wellness  Appreciation  Protection  Comforting A Grieving Heart

No scissors, tape, glue or piping required, all you need is a napkin.
By Arnold D. World

$19.95
ISBN 978-0-9833399-0-8
51995>

9 780983 339908